Books by Jill E. Buffington

Your Dreams Are Who You Are!

It's More Than Just A Hunch!

Creativity is in You!

Where is Happiness?

Dedication

This series is dedicated to my Grandma, Janice Buffington, who gave me the artistic tools and the inspiration to be creative at a very young age. She always provided constructive criticism, constant support and encouragement. Grandma Buffington critiqued all of these illustrations at the age of 95 and passed on a few months later. She will always be my biggest fan.

Special Appreciation

Thank you to my parents, Susan and Rick Buffington who have showered me with love and support my entire life. You have both nurtured all of the creative energies I had as a child, and I am blessed to have your continued support as an adult.

Thank you to the rest of my loving family and friends who have heard about my books for years. Your excitement and support ignited my desire to share Jubi with the world!

Creativity is in You!
Copyright © 2022 by Jill Elisabeth Buffington
Registration #: TXu 2-341-242

Text and Illustrations by Jill E. Buffington
All rights reserved
ISBN: 978-1-955092-01-2

Roaring Light Productions
Somerset, MA 02726
www.jubibooks.com

Printed in the United States of America. No part of this publication may be reproduced or transmitted in any form by any means, graphic, electronic, or mechanical, including photocopying, recording, taping or any information storage or retrieval system, without permission in writing from the publisher.

Creativity is in You!

By: Jill E. Buffington

You are so creative, just as much as another could be.
You have unique ideas - the mind of a visionary!

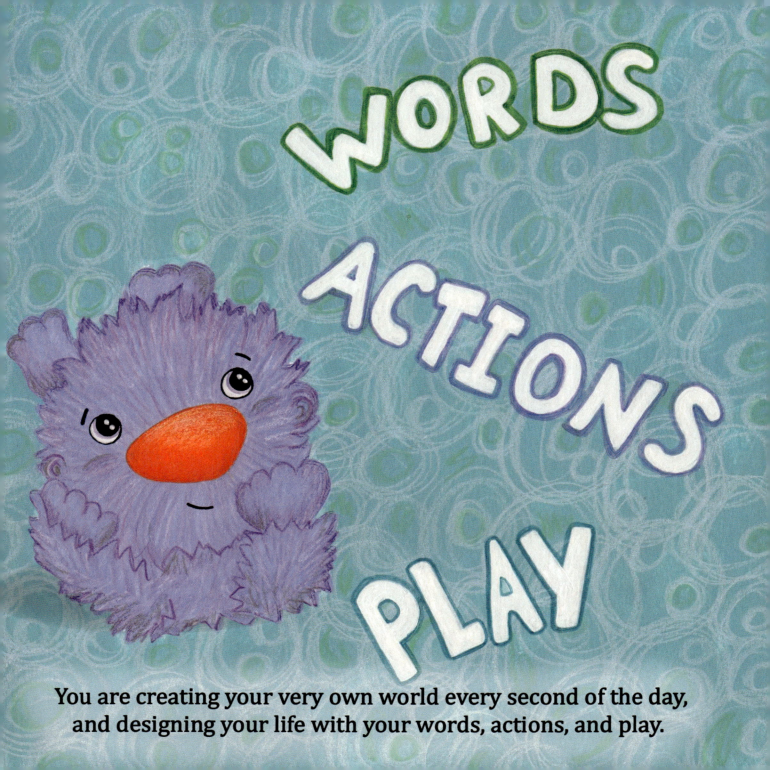

You are creating your very own world every second of the day,
and designing your life with your words, actions, and play.

You are a clever being with the most original thoughts and plans. They can be things you create with your mind or with your hands.

Now take some time to think about what you would like to form.
Let the ideas wash over you, even if they're not the norm.

A creative place could be a spot where no one else would go.
Exploring this grand, wide open space will help your mind to grow.

There are so many ways you can let your creativity shine.
Just stay true to what you love and you'll do just fine.

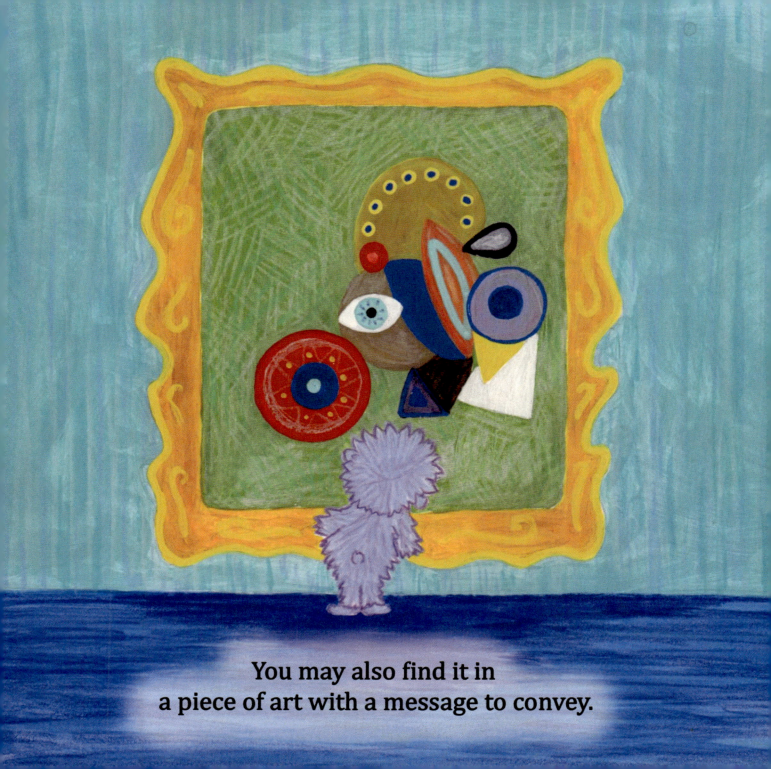

You may also find it in
a piece of art with a message to convey.

Creators build magnificent structures that amaze the modern world.

They also craft super soft sweaters
with patterns and intricate twirls.

Creative folks write interesting articles, maybe a best-selling book.

They even make delicious sauces with veggies for dishes they cook.

Some get so inventive with numbers, charts and graphs.

Others come up with funny jokes, capturing some laughs.

Creativity can be a fantastic and incredibly mystical trick.

You can even be creative with science,
and help those who are sick.

A creative mind is always ready for a challenge to appear.
It's able to take on a difficult task, erasing all doubt or fear.

Over time you will notice this talent comes from observing.
So always keep in mind that you are constantly learning!

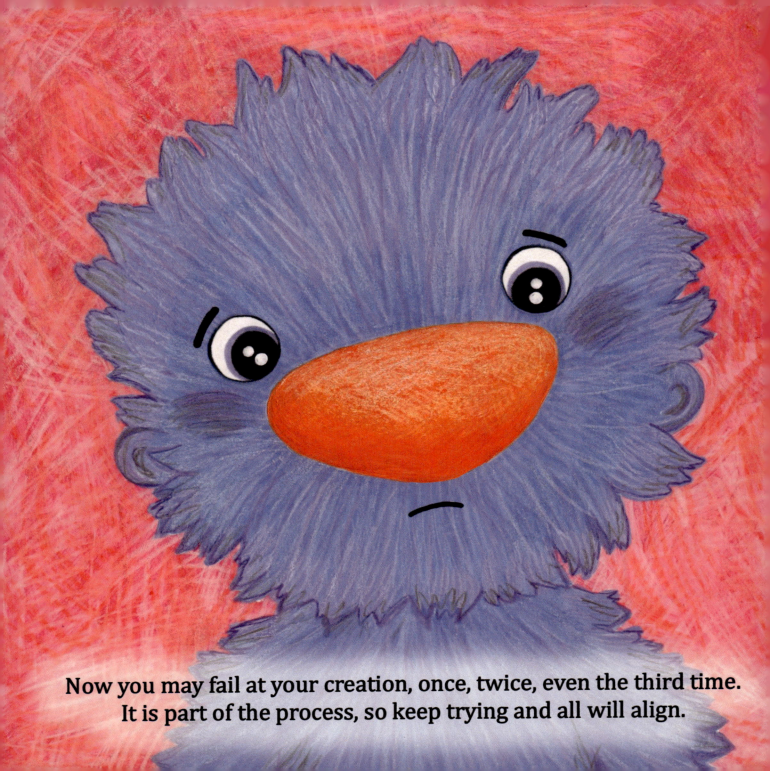

Now you may fail at your creation, once, twice, even the third time.
It is part of the process, so keep trying and all will align.

These problems are only chances hidden in a disguise.
Your creativity will help you through, no matter what the size!

Today is the day to break out of your comfort zone.
Be adventurous and be brave, attempt the wild unknown!

There is so much you can create on this earth,
but make sure to include love, happiness and self-worth.

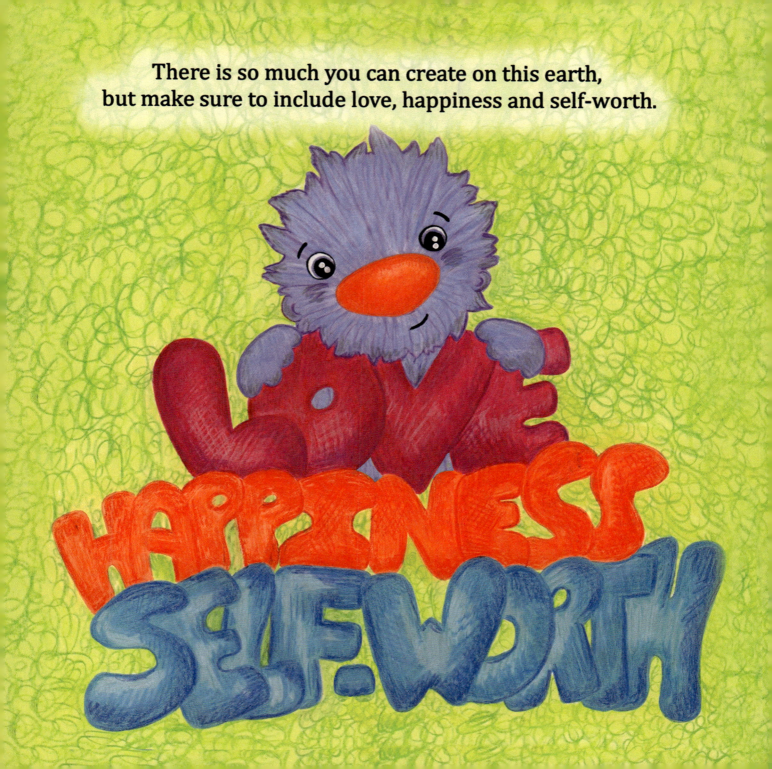

And trust that creativity is absolutely in you, too!

About the Author

Jill Buffington, who was born and raised in New England, lives in a cottage by the ocean with her sweet puppy Dreyfus, and curious kitties, Shamu, Hefner and Gideon. She enjoys snowy and creative winters, and fun-filled beach days in the summer. Jill's first art teacher and the most encouraging person in her artistic journey was her grandmother, who was an artist herself. "My grandmother instilled a strong artistic foundation, as well as many of the creative inspirations I use today." Jill's artistic work includes a combination of residential and commercial paintings, sculptures, book illustrations and jewelry. She has also been a part of community art healing projects across the country.

Jill has also worked in the personal and spiritual development world for over a decade. Her children's book concepts support social-emotional learning by encouraging children to be creative, trust their intuition, choose happiness, and pursue their dreams.

During the illustration process of these books, Jill was excited to use bright colors and whimsical themes. Her fun-loving and furry character "Jubi" (short for "Jubilee") was created so that children can join in with his spirited, child-like wonder while reading the series. "I've always been a creator, almost from the time I could walk. My love of art and my spiritual journey influenced this series." Jill hopes that the vibrant art and heart-felt messages will become an inspiring and meaningful part of all children's lives.

Made in the USA
Middletown, DE
29 July 2023